Civic Skills and Values

Helpfulness

By Dalton Rains

www.littlebluehousebooks.com

Copyright © 2024 by Little Blue House, Mendota Heights, MN 55120. All rights reserved. No part of this book may be reproduced or utilized in any form or by any means without written permission from the publisher.

Little Blue House is distributed by North Star Editions:
sales@northstareditions.com | 888-417-0195

Produced for Little Blue House by Red Line Editorial.

Photographs ©: Shutterstock Images, cover, 4, 7, 8–9, 10, 12–13, 15, 16, 19, 21, 23, 24 (top left), 24 (top right), 24 (bottom left), 24 (bottom right)

Library of Congress Control Number: 2022920145

ISBN
978-1-64619-816-0 (hardcover)
978-1-64619-845-0 (paperback)
978-1-64619-901-3 (ebook pdf)
978-1-64619-874-0 (hosted ebook)

Printed in the United States of America
Mankato, MN
082023

About the Author

Dalton Rains writes and edits nonfiction children's books. He lives in Minnesota.

Table of Contents

A Helping Hand 5

At Home 11

Helping Others 17

Glossary 24

Index 24

A Helping Hand

Helpfulness means doing things for other people. You can do chores like washing the dishes.

Helping can be hard work. After cleaning, you might feel tired.

Other times helping can be fun.

You can help wash a car.

At Home

There are many ways to help at home.

You can mop the floors.

Moms and dads have a lot to do, and you can help them.
You can fold clothes for them.

Brothers and sisters might need help.

You can help your sister make a drawing.

Helping Others

There are other ways to be helpful.

You can help your classmates.

You can help friends. When they feel sad, you can talk to them. You can show them that you care.

You can help your city too. You can pick up trash to clean the park.

There are many ways to be helpful.

Helpfulness makes other people feel good.

Glossary

clothes

mop

drawing

trash

Index

C
car, 8

F
friends, 18

P
park, 20

S
sister, 14